THRIVING WHILE
BLACK

THE ACT OF SURVIVING AND
THRIVING IN THE SAME SPACE

D1402246

CORI J. WILLIAMS MSW L.C.S.W

CKC PUBLISHING HOUSE
L L C

Manufactured in the United States of America

ISBN: 978-0-578-23685-8 (paperback)
ISBN: 978-0-578-23686-5 (ebook)

For information regarding special discounts for
bulk purchases, please contact CKC Publishing
House LLC. at (404) 850-0970
info@ckcpublishinghousellc.com
Atlanta, Georgia

CONTENTS

ACKNOWLEDGEMENTS

There are many people that I wish to acknowledge that have contributed to my success. First, I would like to thank my Lord and Savior Jesus Christ for granting me the wisdom and courage to relentlessly pursue the path that I am on and for fueling my dreams of success. I would like to thank my best friend, my brother Shaun F. Williams, who has always been in my corner and been my biggest cheerleader since day one. His passing in November of 2018 has by far been the most hurtful experience that I have ever endured. I often sit and reminisce about the many conversations that he and I would have about our dreams and aspirations.

His words continue to resonate within me until this very day. He would always tell me, "Cori, don't stop dreaming, and make sure your dreams are so extraordinary and so out of this world that the average mind will never be able to comprehend your viewpoints." My family has always been supportive of all my endeavors. My mother, father, sister, and brother were instrumental in shaping my ideology early in life. We may not have been rich in financial wealth, but we were rich with unconditional love and support.

Lastly, I would like to thank the following people who have directly and indirectly had a positive influence in my life and continue to inspire me until this very day.

Family and those that continue to inspire me:

Anika Moore-Williams (wife), Robert & Delores Williams, Minnie Williams, Feleascia Bridges, The Bowden & Joseph Family, The Shaw Family, The Moore Family and Perkins Family, Jacqueline Wilson LMHC, Dawn Carew, Shamolie Wyckoff MD, Tasmia Henry MD, the Trosclair Family, The entire Williams Family. Kirsten Williams, Diamond Williams, Dj & Deshaun Williams, Claudette Brown, Thomas and Skye Mattison, Kaitlyn, To my brothers Robert (Pete) Paige and Jeff Duffy.

To my greatest inspirations, my children Kayla Williams and Cori Williams Jr.

My Fathers Uplift Inc. Family:

Dr. Charles Clayton Daniels Jr. LICSW, Samantha Fils LCSW, Lakisha R. Austin MBA LICSW, Leonard Tshitenge, George Boakye-Yiadom

Friends:

Jordyn Seide, David Rainer, Mr. & Mrs. Terry Gresham, Mr. & Mrs. Xavier Fairley, Mr. & Mrs. Carl Brown, Janna Ayoub, Annie Canuto

Dedication:

In the memory of my big brother Shaun F. Williams.

INTRODUCTION

*T*hriving *While Black* sets out to explore the psychological and emotional consequences of being Black in corporate America.

From the start, Black people have been discriminated against and excluded based on their skin color. The dehumanization of Black people during slavery is but a shackle that still lies in the background, sneaking up on them and creating the question of where their place is in America.

There still exists a belief that white people are better than Black people and Black people are not equal to white people. There seems to be an unwritten law in America that seeks to ensure that Black citizens remain at the lower rung of the social ladder. Thus, the progression higher up the social ladder reveals the presence of fewer African Americans because they are regarded as the minority. So, even when Black people get top-class qualifications or give their best, it most often does not translate into getting access to the spheres of influence because they are scarcely seen as deserving.

According to a study by Stokely Carmichael and Charles Hamilton in the 1960s, there exists persistent Black inequalities in the structural makeup of America. An average white person, regardless of motivation and behavior, benefits from social structures and organizational patterns that have continually put the average Black person at a disadvantage. These inequalities are not inherent due to differences in the abilities of white and Black people, but instead, due to the differences in access to opportunities between the two groups.

Some white people have tried to assert that success in America is tied to an individual's hard work, and that race does not enhance or impede the upward mobility of individuals. This statement does not acknowledge the systemic and institutionalized forms of racism that ensure that access to opportunities is more available to white individuals. The inability to acknowledge the wide racial gap between Black and white people erases the reality of Black individuals and portrays them as lazy and unwilling to work hard, when the reality is that Black people need to work harder than their white counterparts to achieve the bare minimum in American society.

Furthermore, Black workers in corporate America must grapple with racial microaggressions in the workplace, which often involves white workers assuming that their Black counterparts are inferior to them. As such, being Black in a predominantly white space is getting used to deriding comments as well as compliments for apt and articulate speech, as though achieving a great feat that someone of a Black nature would ordinarily not achieve.

Such statements of awe at the intelligence and oratory skills of a Black person stem from the assumption of intellectual inferiority. Black workers in corporate America are victims of this, where they are passed over when important decisions are being made because of the belief that they have nothing intellectual to bring to the table. This assumption of intellectual inferiority is an obstacle to the upward mobility of a Black person in their organization.

To overcome this and much more, such as the inferiority tag placed on the African American vernacular English, working as a Black individual in corporate America involves code-switching at every point. This forces Black people to live in a contrived duality, always negotiating their humanity and validity by trying to fit into the predominantly white space. Such acts of daily inhabiting of multiple identities and never having the freedom to be oneself can be detrimental to the mental health of an individual.

Black people are Americans too and should not have to be seen as less and unequal! Their humanity should not be reduced to mere negative stereotypes. And there should not be a forced need for Blacks to adopt mainstream white culture and neglect their own African American identity, just to fit into corporate America.

America prides itself on diversity. But the beauty of diversity is not gathering different and diverse people and trying to make them act the same way. Instead, it is bringing diverse people together and allowing their diversity to thrive. This is the focus of this book, and this should be the focus of corporate America.

Cori J. Williams MSW L.C.S.W
Boston, Massachusetts

CHAPTER ONE

SEAT AT THE TABLE

A s a child, I imagined growing up, attending college, getting a degree, and climbing up the social ladder. For me, going to college meant that I would have a better chance at life and that I would be able to live up to my full potential without any restrictions. However, this dream of mine as a child is far from the reality. The progression higher up the social ladder reveals the presence of fewer African Americans. We are regarded as the minority, and this minority position could be seen by some people to be the reason why fewer Black people are found up the social ladder. Some might be quick to say that Black people are lesser than white people in the larger population, and because of this and statistically speaking, there would be a smaller ratio of Black people compared to those who are white in places with a 'random' selection of people. Places like colleges, boardrooms, and basically places of influence; some people may think that placement into these areas of influence is solely based on merit. If you merit it, then you should be there, and thus, the presence of fewer African Americans in these places can be said to be because they did not merit it, but is this true? Before any talk of merit can be discussed, there needs to be a conversation about equality of opportunity. You cannot know whether an individual would merit a position if they never had access to the position in the first place, or have access to positions that would predispose them to exhibiting their inherent capabilities and abilities that would be later suited for the position. Basically, you cannot talk about merit if a certain group of people are limited from exploring their inherent capabilities and potentials. African Americans, from the beginning, have been restricted from exploring their potential, but have instead been weighed down by a cage of stereotypes that has for decades, ensured that they remain at the lower rung of the societal ladder. The few that struggled to squeeze their way through the noose placed around African Americans and managed to climb up further, are still not free from the clutches of stereotypes.

A walk through history

Like I said earlier, there cannot be a conversation about merit and accessibility to the sphere of influence for Black people without a conversation about equal opportunity for them, and for there to be a conversation about equal opportunity, there has to be a walk through African American history. African Americans trace their history to slavery. Black people were brought as slaves to America, and they basically were used by their white slave owners to do menial jobs. These slaves worked in terrible conditions on plantations, as household staffs and service workers. They were involved in plowing the fields, planting, harvesting, and the processing of crops. They were also involved in rearing livestock. They took care of the houses. They worked in factories, and because they were slaves, their labor was unpaid. It is noteworthy to say that the U.S. economy, without the exploitation of Blacks, could not boast of the gains it currently so espouses. According to the 2019 Labor Day Report, the U.S. economy was built on the exploitation and occupational segregation of people of color, and even after the abolishment of slavery, Black people were still not regarded to be equal with white people, and there was a systemic force that ensured that Black citizens did not have access to the same opportunities as white citizens. They were encouraged to continue working for the families that had previously enslaved them. Some laws were enacted, specifically the Jim Crow law in the south, to ensure that Black people remained only as workers in domestic and farming positions. Up till this day, and even with the proclamation that Black people could work wherever they wanted, as long as they were qualified, we still see fewer Black people in positions of influence. It is not enough to say that slavery is no more, and that Black people are free. A person cannot be free if he is caged. A person cannot be free when they are not given access to opportunities. A person cannot be free when they are still reduced to unfounded stereotypes, and this has been the reality of African Americans for decades.

Would running faster make you gain more ground?

Anthony Carvevale, a research professor at Georgetown University, said that minorities are running faster but losing ground to white Americans. This comment was made after Georgetown University conducted a study that revealed that despite the level of education attained by people of color, there still exists a large racial inequality in job opportunities for people of color, compared to white Americans. This study clearly expresses the reality that minorities face in America. It is not enough to give your best, because your best most often does not translate into you getting access to the spheres of influence. There is an unwritten law in America that seeks to ensure that Black people remain at the lower rung of the social ladder, and thus Black people have remained in positions they have been inhabiting since slavery. People might be quick to dismiss this and say that it is a delusion of the Black mind, and that Black people only need to work harder, go to college, and get degrees, and that these are enough to get them a seat at the table. However, this study at Georgetown University showed that the social standing of African Americans and Latinos does not increase despite going to college. Being a minority and college graduate does not automatically mean that you would be seen better than a minority high school dropout. It is as though, in American society, there is a fixated and institutionalized idea of Black people as niggers, violent, loud, and not human enough. That idea doesn't seem to shift, even when the Black person goes to college and proves otherwise. This doesn't mean that Black citizens who didn't go to college should be regarded as less, but you might think that the reason Black people don't get their due is because of the implicit human bias that sees someone as more deserving based on their qualifications. However, for Black people, even with their qualifications, are scarcely seen as deserving. There are more white Americans holding better jobs than Black

Americans. And even for Black college graduates with similar qualifications as their white peers, we see them being passed over for their white counterparts. An average white worker with an entry-level education is likely to earn more than a Black worker with an entry-level education. A report showed that in 2016, 77 percent of the good jobs were held by white workers, despite the fact that they represented 69 percent of available job holders, while Black workers had 10 percent of the good jobs, out of the 13 percent of jobs they held. What this means is that white workers hold more jobs generally than Black workers, and out of the jobs they held, they had better placement in good jobs than Black workers. However, there is an over representation of Black workers in jobs that do not require college degrees. More Black people tend to be in menial job positions. If truly there exists equality of access, we should see an equal or near equal ratio of white workers to Black workers in the good jobs that require college degrees. It is noteworthy to say that America is designed to ensure that fewer Black citizens make it to college. This of course is not contained in the law, but rather is an unwritten ethos in society.

The racial gaps between Black and white people seem to be ever widening. In a report by Philip Mazzocco, the infant mortality rate among Black people is 130 percent higher than white people. The average life span of a Black person is 3.6 years lower than a white person. There is an implicit bias in healthcare that affects the treatment a Black person receives. There is the belief, which has been fostered by research, that Black people have a higher tolerance for pain compared to white people. This belief has led to the delayed treatment Black citizens receive in healthcare, which invariably leads to more health complications and death from these complications. The median household income as stated by Philip Mazzocco, puts Black households to earn 57 percent less income than white households. The poverty rate among Black citizens is 146 percent higher than white citizens. Home ownership rates of Black people are 61 percent lower that white home ownership. These inequalities are not inherent due to differences in the abilities of Black and white people, but instead due to differences in the access to opportunities between the two groups. Black people have less connection and hence have less access to jobs. And even for those who manage to get a job, they are still treated unequally regarding wages. Reports show that as a worker's level of education increases, wage discrimination reduces between white people and minorities. However, the difference still exists in wages. Also, the average Black child experiences less upward mobility than white children. A research study showed that for every one hundred Black children who grow up in the bottom fifth of the income distribution, less than three will make it to the top fifth as adults, while white children are four times likely to move from the bottom to the top fifth. The study also found that Black children were more likely to experience downward mobility than their white counterparts. The study estimated that less than one in ten Black children growing up at the top of the social ladder would stay there as adults.

There is also a growing inequality in the number of Black people in the field of science in America. The image of a Black scientist has historically been something that white America could not conceive due to the assumed inferiority of the average Black man. The field of science is an important one and has formed the basis of the development in the world today. In the 1980s, Black people accounted for only 2.3 percent of employed scientists and engineers. This racial inequality still exists today. Some might say that the low number of Black people in the field of science and engineering is an indicator of the inferior status of the African man. However, the reason for this is not far-fetched. Take for instance Angela, a young smart girl who was in the gifted program in middle school. Upon entering high school, she goes to see her high school counselor who is a white man with a balding head and large rimmed glasses. He asks her what she would like to become, and she says a physicist. This counselor, without looking at her impeccable records, tells her that her dream was too high and that she should settle for something less ambitious, like the arts. Angela is surprised, because all her life she wanted to be a physicist and believed she was smart enough to become one, but here was her college counselor telling her otherwise. For him, there was no way a Black girl was smart enough to become a physicist. Even Black boys are faced with such stereotypes. There are a lot of promising young Black kids who want to venture into the field of science and technology, but due to the implicit bias that Black people are not smart enough, they get sidelined and are forced to choose a different field of study. For those that struggle through high school and college and manage to get into graduate school, some drop out due to feelings of self-doubt. An average Black person that manages to get into graduate school discovers that he is either the only Black person in his class or among the few. Wanting to prove that he deserves to be in that room puts an unnecessary strain on him. It exacerbates the feelings of insecurity which could possibly lead to him to dropping out. This sadly is the reality of most Black people and hence explains the reduced number of Black people in science and technology.

The effect of slavery and Jim Crow laws is yet to lose its grip on Black lives. Black slaves were not allowed access to education and were thus denied the opportunity to maximize their potential and to make more wealth for themselves. And even after the abolishment of slavery, there was a restriction of Black citizens to menial jobs, which barely offered them enough to feed their families, let alone send their kids off to school. There was also the segregation in schools that discriminated Black workers from white workers, where white students were seen as smarter, better, and had more potential for success than the Black workers, and this resulted into feelings of inferiority among the Black students. This, coupled with the fact that an average Black student sees fewer Black people going to college and attaining prominence. It is not enough to dream big, because dreaming big and working to achieve that would not lessen the discriminate treatment of Black people. The dream of an average Black child is not to go to college, get a degree, and be at the top in their field, but to be alive. An average Black child, is from a young age, given the lecture by his parents on how he is likely to be seen and treated differently just because of his skin color. And thus, a Black child strives to survive and sees ambition as a luxury he cannot afford.

Contributions of African Americans to the development of America

Social media was thrown into an uproar in June of 2020, when an article about the possibility of Beethoven being Black surfaced the internet. There, however, is no concrete evidence for this, but the mere speculation that Beethoven could be Black was both a thing of joy and outrage in the Black community. Several people started highlighting the history of whitewashing in Europe and America. The racial origin of Beethoven has not yet been identified, but some people asked an interesting question: if Beethoven were Black, would his music have gotten the critical acclaim it did?

African Americans and their contribution to present day America has surely been erased by our history books. Jacquelyn Derouselle wrote a piece on the contributions of African American slaves to the development of America. In the piece, she mentioned that enslaved African Americans' labor was essential for the survival of European colonies' economies in America, from the 16th century to the 19th century. It is estimated that slaveholders extracted over $14 trillion dollars' worth of labor from their captives. In her piece, Derouselle wrote that slaves brought with them the knowledge of growing rice to South Carolina and Georgia and taught slave owners how to cultivate the crop.

African Americans also contributed to American Evolution. The prospect of freedom encouraged many African Americans to take part in the war. Reports show that by 1783, thousands of Black Americans had become involved in the war. Some were able to secure their freedom by partaking in the war for America's independence. Due to the difficulty to fill in enlistment quotas, states began to turn to slaves as manpower for the war. Slaves were promised their freedom if they fought in the war. There is no denying the role African Americans played in American evolution; however, their contributions were swept under the rug. The Declaration of Independence promised liberty for all men but failed to put an end to slavery.

African Americans contributed immensely to the field of medicine despite being excluded and discriminated against. The American Medical Association (AMA), which was founded in 1846, for years prevented African Americans from being members of the association based strictly on skin color. Alexander T. Augusta, Charles B. Purvis, and Alpheus W. Tucker in 1869 were denied admission into the American Medical Association despite being eligible for admission. The reason for the denial was that the association did not admit Black physicians. The AMA further refused to consult with Black physicians and excluded them from educational opportunities on the account of skin color. In response to being excluded, African Americans created their own medical organizations, and despite the level of discrimination they endured, they were still able to make significant contributions. Ernest John, an African American man, was born in Charleston, South Carolina in 1883, and his ideas on cell membrane activity was of immense contribution to the field of science, as it completely changed the prevailing scientific opinion of his time. John received a bachelor's degree with honors from Dartmouth. While in college, he developed an interest in biology. He particularly was interested in the structure and development of cells. His ideas on cell membrane were able to demonstrate that a cell's cytoplasm and ectoplasm are equally as important as the nucleus in heredity. During his career, he published over 60 research papers and two books. He, however, did not gain recognition in America. There is also Percy Julian who was born in Alabama in 1899. Reports showed that Julian discovered cortisone from soybean oil, which was a cheap and effective treatment of arthritis. He also was the first to synthesize physostigmine, which was important in the treatment of glaucoma. He also was the first to synthesize hormones, which greatly reduced the prices of drugs for people who could not afford expensive natural drugs. He was the first Black person to be offered the post of chief chemist and director of research position for the Glidden Company in Chicago. Charles Drew was an African American medical doctor whose research on separating and storing blood, in addition to his research on blood plasma, was essential in saving lives during World War II. He was also one of the first Black people to become a diplomat in surgery. In addition, Drew was the first Black person to be appointed an examiner by the American Board of Surgery. There are other Black medical professionals whose names have vanished into obscurity despite their immense contribution to the field of medical science and technology.

African Americans and American Music

What would American music be like without Black influences? It is impossible for there to be a conversation about American music without examining the origins and impact of Black music. There exists in American music today the overarching influence of Black music that can be felt in every chord and lyric. Black music is the defining point of American music. When slaves were brought to America, their music and cultures came with them. From Jazz to Blues, to Rock 'N' Roll, to Hip-Hop, and Black pop music, there is no denying how pervasive these music genres are in the American consciousness. "Hip Hop music with its drums, bass has altered the kind of pop music Americans listen to," writes Mac Dressman. Black music is tagged as songs of struggle and spirit, as it was born out of the need to be heard. This has been the revolutionary factor about these songs, as they extend beyond mere stringing of words, beats, and tunes, but are instead rooted in the unique experiences of being Black and being human. Blues for instance, due to its dynamic and diverse nature and its use of readily available instruments, made it accessible to all people, regardless of their socio-economic status or race. Black people were able to create their own music at a time when they were denied seats at the American table, and the music that they created would for years dictate and guide the American music culture. There are many African American artists today, who are constantly defining the course of American music and making American music the center of the world's music.

African Americans, despite being undervalued and constantly discriminated against, were in the face of these difficulties, being able to achieve great feat themselves. This, however, is not enough, as America is still far from being accommodating of Blacks. There are still fewer Black people at the table, and for the few that have managed to gain access to corporate America, that access came at a price, and sadly, has not reduced the level of discrimination they receive. Black actors and artists who have gained critical acclaim are still being sidelined and not getting the necessary awards they deserve. A seat at the table should be one that is accessible to Black people if they merit it.

CHAPTER TWO

I AM NOT MY SKIN. I AM NOT MY HAIR (FINDING COMFORT IN ONE'S SKIN)

A random Google search on "professional hairstyle" would bring well curated images of white women with long straight or wavy hair. Another search on "unprofessional hairstyle" would bring images of Black women wearing their natural hairstyles. This occurrence threw the internet into a pandemonium with lots of women sharing their stories of racial discrimination based on hairstyles in the corporate world.

To an outsider, and by outsider, I am referring to non-Black people or individuals who have not had phenomenological experiences of racial discrimination based on hairstyles, the pandemonium that occurred might seem like an overreaction. "Is not there meant to be a standard for appearance in the corporate environment?" they might ask. "You cannot wear whatever you want to wear to an office," some might add. But the uproar about racial discrimination based on hairstyle is not merely a matter of preference or choice, but instead, is a systemic problem that targets only a fraction of individuals. The policy against certain hairstyles might to some individuals apply equally to every individual, but when these hairstyles are worn primarily by a certain group of individuals, then the ban is targeted. If a ban against straight hair is implemented in corporate America, the race that would primarily be affected will be those with naturally occurring straight hair. This is the case with discrimination against the Afro, dreadlocks, braids, and cornrows.

In 2010, Chastity Jones was offered a job as a customer service representative in a catastrophe management firm. Her job was to interface with clients who had complaints. The firm, however, was worried about her dreadlocks and requested that she cut her locks. Jones refused and lost the job offer. Jones, who felt cheated and discriminated against, decided to file a suit against the firm. However, she lost the suit.

Black people have for decades faced different forms of discrimination based on their skin color. From a young age, a Black child is made to feel different based on their skin color. Male and female people of color deal with stereotypes and are forced daily to prove their humanity. Black females are faced with a different form of discrimination based on their choice to wear their hairstyles naturally. A Black woman is faced with multiple oppressions. A Black woman is discriminated against for being Black and for being a woman. The experiences of multiple interacting oppressions differ from being oppressed for being Black and for being a woman. This form of oppression is not an aggregate form of oppression but instead an interacting and overlapping form of oppression that differs distinctly from being Black and for being a woman. Some organizations pride themselves in being diverse, owing to their employment of Black and female staff. However, the majority of employed Black staff are males, and most of the employed female staff are white. This form of oppression is tagged as intersectionality and was put forward by Professor Kimberlé Williams Crenshaw to explain the oppression faced by Black women. Corporate America boasts of a smaller number of Black female executives, and for the few Black female executives, discrimination based on hairstyles is prevalent.

In 2016, there was an uproar in Black communities in the United States after a Black woman, Attica Scott, took to Twitter to complain that her daughter, Ashanti Scott, was sent home from school due to her hairstyle. The school, Butler High School in Louisville, Kentucky had a policy that hair must always be clean and neat. Ashanti Scott had worn her hair naturally to school and was sent home because her hair was deemed extreme, distracting, and attention seeking. This policy, however, seemed to target just Black women. A recent study found that 80 percent of Black women felt pressured to switch their hairstyles to align with Eurocentric standards. In 2007, Ashley Baker, in New York City, gave a presentation titled, The Dos and Don'ts of Corporate Fashion. She had a slide of a Black woman with an afro hairstyle with the caption, "Say no to the fro." She also, in the same presentation said, "How dreadful," while referring to the dreadlocks. For the acclaimed fashion experts, black hairstyles are deemed as not stylish enough. Adjectives like dirty, messy, and unprofessional have been used to describe naturally occurring hairstyles among Black women. Women who are faced with double othering based on their skin color and their choice of hair, are burdened with anxiety about who they are, and are forced to change an important part of themselves to be accepted by the society in which they live.

Climbing up the social ladder is harder for people of color, and staying up there is even harder. The chances of you remaining up on the ladder is dependent on how willing you are to erase your Blackness and conform to western values. A Black person needs to learn how to be white in order to survive and thrive in America.

Centuries ago, western scientists and philosophers believed that there existed a hierarchy in humanity. This hierarchy placed different human races into groups based on cranial features, skin color, and hairstyle. At the top of this hierarchy was the Europeans with their white skin color, pointed noses, and straight long hair. The Europeans were believed to be closer to God. At the bottom of this hierarchy, closer to the animals, was the Black race. With this classification came a further distinction between the races.

The Black race was seen to be barbaric, savages with animal impulses. They were also tagged as ugly, while the white race was tagged as beautiful and intellectually superior. The white man believed that the Black race needed salvation, and for this to be achieved, the Black race had to be assimilated into the white way of life. This of course meant a total erasure of everything Black, and a forced compliance to everything white. This prejudice against the Black race has formed the basis of racial discrimination faced by Black people in present day America. There cannot be a conversation about systemic racism without a conversation about slavery and the ideologies that led to slavery. African slaves brought to America were faced with dehumanization. Psychologists for decades have studied how dehumanization leads to the cruel acts meted out on certain individuals. The act of seeing another human as non-human gives a basis for acts of cruelty done against them. For an oppressor to oppress an individual without feeling guilty, they would need to sever any link that might connect them to the oppressed, and this of course involves seeing them as less human. Admitting to yourself that an individual is like you would bring about internal tension because this admittance of the humanity of the other individual would lead to an admittance of your inhumane acts against them. Seeing Black individuals and their way of life as barbaric and animalistic provided the white supremacists enough justification for their acts against them. This lack of admittance of the humanity of the Black race made the white supremacists believe that Black people needed to be assimilated into the white way of life. Several African slaves brought to America were forced by their slave owners to shave off their hair. This was part of the dehumanization of Black people. Black female slaves with kinky hair were forced to cover their hair and work in the fields, while those with looser hair texture that bordered on the Caucasian hair texture, were used as domestic slaves and were also forced to conform to white standards. There also have been reports of Black slaves who wore their hairstyles in elaborate styles, being forced to cover them due to the attention from white men the hair brought them.

The politics of Black hair in present day America

In the 1960s, there was a surge in the number of women wearing their hair in Afro style. Angela Davis is one of such women who advocated for the wearing of an afro as she herself is seen wearing her hair naturally. In today's America, the choice of wearing your hair naturally is seen to be a political statement and a way of reclaiming your identity as a Black woman, rejecting the Eurocentric standards of beauty that subjugates all things Black. This labeling of women who wear their hair naturally as political and revolutionary causes them to face discrimination in the corporate world. Discrimination against natural hair in the corporate environment is beyond a mere fashion statement, but instead a systemic policing of the choices and identity of Black women.

In today's America, Black women of high social standing are often seen wearing their hair straight, as this is the only way to ensure that they climb the social ladder with less difficulty than their counterparts who choose to wear their hair naturally. Women who choose to wear their hair naturally are seen as masculine and radical, and in corporate America, white people tend to be more self-conscious around such women, based on the stereotypes attached to the hairstyles.

Young Black girls in today's America are raised to see the hair which grows naturally from their head as ugly and dirty, and they are made by their mothers to undergo hair straightening, using chemicals or hot combs. For the average Black mother, her daughter faces enough discrimination in America based on her skin color alone, and adding another form of discrimination through the choice of wearing your hair naturally is out of the question. So, a Black mother who seeks to ensure that her daughter has a slim chance of surviving in America, removes the kinks in her hair. Studies revealed that Black women who wear their hair naturally face discrimination from their Black counterparts. This discrimination is of course a result of internalized racism. Growing up Black and surviving involves the internalization of white standards.

Why is hair so important?

Our identity as individuals come from various aspects of our lives. Our work, gender, race, age, religion, and sexual orientation are factors which we or others use in defining us. Identity is formed through how we view ourselves in the world and how others view us. Sociologist, Herbert Mead, conceptualizes three aspects of identity: how we see ourselves, how we think others see us, and how we are truly. An individual tends to rely more on the first two in defining his identity. We see ourselves in a particular way and we integrate how we think others see us into our self-concept, which we use in defining ourselves.

We live in a social world, and a huge part of this world is social interactions. From walking on the streets to going to work to buying groceries, individuals engage in a form of interaction, and as these interactions occur, we form perceptions about others based on certain cues we observe. These perceptions are integral for a fluid interaction. Through the way a person talks and dresses, we allow ourselves to form opinions about who or what they are. Certain aspects of an individual's behavior offer us an insight into who they are, and we use these insights as a basis of interaction. Skin color and hairstyles are central to an individual's sense of identity. The skin color and hair texture of Black people are inextricably linked to being Black, and any structural attempt at policing certain parts of this is an attempt to police an individual's sense of self. The texture of Black hair made it possible for the hair to be sculpted into various shapes and forms. In early African civilizations, hair was more than just a beauty mechanism, but instead possessed cultural significance. African hair was a symbol of pride and spirituality. It also provided a sense of community for individuals. Different ethnic groups in African society had different hairstyles which was a marker of identity and provided for individuals a sense of group belonging. From the hairstyle an individual wore, you could tell who they were. Hair was a marker of status. With slavery came the erasure of the cultural identity of Black people, as slaves were forced to either shave off their hair or cover it. Even with the end of slavery, Black women were still forced to cover their hair. As the years went by, what was once a source of pride to the Black race became something shameful.

During slavery, Black women were subject to forced sexual intercourse by white slave owners, which resulted in the birth of mix-raced children who had lighter skin and straighter hair. However, the mixed-race children were not exempt from racist discrimination, even though they were treated better than their Black counterparts with darker skin and kinky hairstyles. This led to a preference in Black people to have straighter hair, due to the belief that they would be treated better.

Studies have shown how the perception of individuals about a person changes depending on the nature of their hair. Participants were shown an image of a Black woman with her natural hair and another image of her with straight hair, and the subjects were more likely to see the straight hair image more positively. One woman, two different hairstyles and two different reactions. This shows how people discriminate based on hair type. Professionalism in the white corporate world is inextricably linked to Eurocentric standards, and for an individual to be considered professional, they must approximate themselves to be the nearest version of the Eurocentric ideals.

Stereotypes have been a field of study in psychology for decades. In 1984, psychologists Susan Fiske and Shelley Taylor introduced the term cognitive miser. They claimed that the human mind is prone to cognitive miserliness and this refers to the mind's tendency to think and solve problems in a less effortful way. One way this happens is through the use of stereotypes. The human mind is unable to deal with complexity, and hence relies on simplistic and reductionist methods in approaching the social world. We see a group of people a certain way based on group membership and the possession of certain features. The fault with this is that it fails to see individuals as humans, and merely reduces them to certain aspects of themselves which most of the time is wrong and misguided. Prejudice against hair and skin color stems from this lack of regard for the complexity that exists in the world.

Reducing Black women to their skin color and their hairstyles burdens them with unfounded stereotypes and robs them of their humanity and individual distinctness. The seam of American society today has been eaten deep by reductionist thinking, which believes that an individual is a certain way based on their skin color and hairstyles.

Hair discrimination is a ubiquitous phenomenon in corporate America, as it robs women of the access to opportunities that should have been theirs, just because a certain part of their identity is laden with negative stereotypes. Present day America would proffer acceptability on a Black person based on how willing they are at erasing their Blackness and conforming to the western standard of beauty.

A look at mainstream media's portrayal of Black professional women would show images of women with long straight hair, while poor, struggling women in unprofessional jobs would wear their hair naturally. This of course leads to the further reinforcement of the belief that the choice to straighten your hair would provide you access to corporate America. For young girls who are exposed to this type of media, they grow up with the belief that natural hair signifies ugly, dirty, and unprofessional, while straight hair signifies beauty and professionalism. This of course is founded in reductionist stereotype. A woman's choice of hairstyle does not in any way reflect her intellectual capacity, neither does it make her more or less professional. Instead, these stereotypes are rooted in the desire for the white people to maintain superiority over Black populations. The consequence of hair discrimination for women of color leads to harmful psychological consequences. Constantly hearing that your natural hair is ugly, unprofessional, or not feminine enough can lead to an internalization of these criticisms which leads to an impaired sense of self.

Even among the Black community, there still exist a preference for straight hair among females and even males. Some Black men prefer Black women with long straightened hair. Marketing ads via TV, social media, and print, have distorted the perspectives of many of Black men about Black women with natural hair. For Black women, these images lead to them not loving who they see in the mirror. In the words of one of my female colleagues who was expressing her outrage about the preference for straightened hair among the Black community, "Are we looking at ourselves through our own African ancestry lens or through a white European lens? Have we become so programmed to not see ourselves in our brothers and sisters who have made choices to live a lifestyle that goes against what one would consider normal?"

There are so many factors that contribute to an average Black professional woman's intersectionality, and when she encounters a lack of love from Black men who do not understand or even acknowledge her struggles as a Black professional woman, it further fuels the opportunity for self-doubt, a lack of self-love, and an overwhelming need to fit in to be accepted by the very community that should love them unconditionally.

I am not my hair. I am not my skin.

This phrase above does not refer to the rejection of Black skin or Black natural hair, but instead, it is a rejection of the negative stereotypes attached to these key features of Black identity. There are women whose choice to wear their hair naturally is a matter of preference and not due to any political reason. And there are also women whose choice to straighten their hair is a matter of fashion and not because they are choosing to conform to Eurocentric beauty standards and rejecting their Black heritage. Historically, Black hair had cultural and political significance, but that has evolved today. Reducing a woman to mere stereotypes based on how she chooses to style her hair is cognitively and intellectually lazy and reflects the need to see the world through the lens of overly simplistic ideals.

There needs to be an espousal of the fact that the choice of hairstyle a woman chooses to wear should not in any way determine the way that she would be treated in the society or limit her access to opportunities. There are no psychological traits attached to texture of hair. American society needs to learn to divorce individuals' choices of hairstyle from their perception of them. A Black professional woman should not have to worry about whether her choice of hairstyle would prevent her from getting that promotion or that job or being treated with decency.

It is important for the average Black female professional to feel at home in her own skin and not be made uncomfortable by her choice to wear her hair in a particular fashion. Finding comfort in one's skin needs a complete embrace of your identity as a Black woman. There needs to be a revolution in corporate America that divorces those harmful and negative stereotypes from certain features of the Black identity.

CHAPTER THREE

I DO NOT SEE COLOR

Kevin Richardson is a 42-year-old African American male who resides in the city of Charlotte, North Carolina with his two children, ages 14 (daughter) and 8 (son). Kevin was born in a rural town in Albany, Georgia during a time in which one's experience with discrimination was so frequent that many had become desensitized to news of racial tension in his town or even hate crime offenses toward other minorities. Kevin was raised by his single mother after witnessing his father's untimely death from a heart condition at the age of seventeen. This event rocked his world and left a huge void in the heart of Kevin throughout his early adulthood. Kevin moved to Charlotte after finishing his computer engineering graduate degree in 2005. Kevin was

CORI J. WILLIAMS MSW LCSW

always told that the city of Charlotte was the perfect place to transition to for up and coming Black professionals. That is where he met his wife Tina while out on the town one evening with his friends. Although Kevin had been predisposed to racial violence back in his hometown, he never experienced any racially motivated attacks against him firsthand.

Kevin started working for an immensely popular tech company in Charlotte. The racial makeup in this company mirrored the town that Kevin grew up in. Upper management positions down to junior analyst positions consisted predominantly of Caucasian males as the company boasted its efforts for their recent establishment of their diversity inclusion program. Kevin was very skilled in his craft and aspired of one day starting his own consulting firm. During his employment at the tech company, Kevin was privy to hearing the many indirect and direct jokes and conversations sprinkled with racial undertones during company outings and at the water cooler by his Caucasian colleagues. Although Kevin would identify his experience at this company as that of a single grain of pepper in a sea of salt, Kevin remained laser focused on trying to climb the ladder in this company. After several years with the company, he eventually did earn a position as project manager.

Kevin would often visit his hometown, bringing his children to visit their grandmother. He wanted to show his children where he grew up in an effort to prompt their appreciation for the things they have. Kevin also wanted to teach his children about the harsh realities of discrimination and racism that continued to plague American, but more importantly his hometown. Kevin celebrated his new promotion with his family and knew in his heart that he had bust his ass to earn that promotion. Kevin also knew the jealousy that began to stir up among his colleagues, since recently being told by another minority colleague that they had overheard other colleagues saying that Kevin "only got the position due to affirmative action." Hearing this only reminded Kevin of his college days at the University of Georgia (UGA) where he excelled in his major, graduating top 3 of his cohort. Kevin was one of only two African Americans in his cohort and had become all too familiar with the nasty stares and side talks coming from the white students. As much as he made every effort to ignore the various microaggressive situations during his college years, these situations planted the seed of self-doubt within him, which left Kevin questioning his worthiness whenever there was an accomplishment.

Kevin also contributes his feelings of unworthiness to the loss of his father during a vital time in his life. Kevin often found himself reflecting on what his life would have been like if his father had not passed. He felt that he walked through life pretending to be a lion only to go home to the comfort of his home to be the lamb he felt he really was inside.

Kevin's story above is one among the many stories of discrimination faced by Black people in corporate America. Navigating corporate America and other spaces that are predominantly white is often a source of discomfort for a person of color. You are faced with subtle forms of racism which makes you question if the action was racist or if you are just being overly sensitive. Some individuals might say that America has risen above prejudice and discrimination, and that individuals who cry out about forms of racism that are not overt and otherwise brutal as it was in the past, were choosing to be victims. You might say that slavery has been abolished and that Black people in America can be whoever they want to be if they work hard. Some might point out the fact that America has had its first black president to indicate that we are in a post-racism era. However, prejudice and discrimination against Black people and other people of color has not ended. It has instead morphed into more subtle forms of racism which are as harmful or even more harmful, overt, and brutal, due to the lack of admittance by American society of its existence. The black skin is laden with a history of oppression, and American society with the intent of eliminating racism, seemed to have adopted a more subtle form of racism which has been tagged as microaggressions.

Many well intending white Americans use the phrase "I do not see color" to indicate that they are not racist and that they see firstly an individual's humanity and not their race. This statement, even though is well intentioned, is subtly harmful. We do not live in a color-blind world, and even if you claim you do not see color, which of course is impossible unless you are color blind, society is not color blind. Saying you do not see color does not in any way reduce racism but instead ignores it. The first step in the attempt at curbing discrimination based on race would be an admittance to the existent of racial disparity, and this cannot occur if an individual, though well-intentioned, claims to not see color.

Take for instance this scenario:

Nicole Bradley is a 24-year-old Caucasian female, raised in a household that was filled with love and pride for their Irish culture. Nicole attended Simmons College in Boston, Massachusetts completing her graduate studies in social work. She recalls days at the dinner table with her family in which discussions on topics ranging from politics and racial tensions amongst other topics, typically resulted in disagreements, due to her father's archaic way of thinking, as she would describe it. Growing up in a rural area of Massachusetts, in which the population was predominantly white, Nicole had little friends that were minorities. In fact, Nicole did not engage with many minorities on a consistent basis until she attended college.

Her encounters while in school have redefined the perspective she once had of minorities, which she contributed to early influences of her father. After graduating, Nicole and a close friend, who is African American, transitioned to a full-time position at a private therapy practice. This therapy practice was located in a predominantly Black community, ran by a predominantly Black staff and management. Nicole and her friend completed their practicum at the same private practice before they both were offered full-time positions there.

During a staff meeting, there were in depth discussions about the plight of the population that the agency served, and Nicole being the only white staff, would at times feel uncomfortable during some of the candid conversations. One day while taking a lunch break, Nicole's friend asked her how she felt about some of the conversations, as well as asked about her feelings regarding a recent client who requested to be transferred from Nicole's care due to not feeling the "cultural connection" with

Nicole. Nicole replied that she felt fine, and when it came to serving the community, she did not wish to judge them based on the premise that she was white. Nicole continued to reflect on the matter and ended the conversation stating, "I don't see color anyway!"

Due to Nicole's 'inability' to see color as she claimed, made it difficult for her to be empathetic towards her Black clients. An important factor of clinical therapy is being able to see things from the perspective of your client, and that involves allowing yourself to be in their shoes and understanding how certain parts of themselves, like race, gender, and sexuality can impact their experiences and how they navigate the world. Choosing to not see color would erase those experiences that people of color face because of their skin color. The client who asked to be transferred from Nicole must have felt that she disregarded their unique experiences as being Black in America.

Claiming to not see color ignores the discrimination faced by people of color for their skin color. Claiming to not see color erases decades of inhumane treatment Black people have faced. Individuals who claim to be from diverse backgrounds are quick to make such comments about not seeing color, and this claim is a form of microaggression as it refuses to acknowledge the oppression of Black people based on their skin color. This insistence by white people to not see color is a way of saying they can never be racists. This, however, is myopic, as the mere act of saying you do not see color is in fact racist. Making the statement of not seeing color grants these individuals a form of moral superiority, which of course can be equated to white superiority, as it denies and invalidates the reality of Black individuals.

There are other forms of microaggression faced by Black individuals in America. A common one is the question of the origin of a Black person. Where are you really from? This question stems from the belief that people of color have origins other than America and have simply just migrated there. For a person of color faced with this question, feelings of unease set in. I am American, and I was born here, but why is there an assumption that I must come from somewhere? Some Black people have faced more blatant forms of this microaggression when they are told to go back to Africa.

There is also the statement by some white people that success in America is tied to an individual's hard work and that race does not enhance or impede the upward mobility of individuals. This statement does not acknowledge the systemic and institutionalized forms of racism that ensure that access to opportunities is more available to white individuals.

There is still a wide racial gap between Black and white people in America, and not acknowledging this erases the reality of Black individuals and portrays them as lazy and unwilling to work hard, when the reality is that Black people need to work harder than their white counterparts to achieve the barest minimum in American society.

A study by American Counseling Association identified some forms of microaggressions faced by Black employees in corporate America.

Assumption of intellectual inferiority.

Hakeem works in an advertising agency, and he is among the only two Black employees there. During his lunch break one day, Hakeem and a few of his white counterparts gathered around in a friendly banter. One of the female colleagues who was white began asking everyone where they went to college, but when it got to Hakeem's turn, she skipped him. Hakeem wanting to know why she skipped him called her out and asked her. "I just assumed you did not go to college," she replied Hakeem. His female colleague felt that just because Hakeem was Black, he possibly could not have gone to college. The irony of this is that the agency only hired people with college degrees, but the implicit bias about Black people overshadowed this fact, and made this white worker assume that Hakeem was just a high school dropout.

Being Black in a predominantly white space is getting used to deriding comments and jeers from colleagues, and sometimes getting used to being complimented when you talk well and are articulate, as though you have achieved a great feat that someone of your nature would not have achieved. "You speak so well." "You are so articulate." "Where did you learn to talk like this?" Black people in predominantly white spaces have heard varying forms of these statements. And to the speakers, there is nothing wrong in their statements. "What harm is there in giving a compliment to another human?" some might ask. The problem with this is not the statement itself but instead the assumption behind it. Black individuals for decades have been deemed as intellectually inferior, and this formed the basis of their denial to educational opportunities. Statements of awe at the intelligence and oratory skills of a Black person stem from this assumption of intellectual inferiority. Being surprised by the intelligence of a Black person is a microaggression because it means that you are working with the notion that this individual is not intelligent. You had, in your mind, placed them at the lowest rung on the intelligence ladder, and them exceeding your expectations shocks you.

Black workers in corporate America are victims of this, where they are passed over when important decisions are being made because of the belief that they have nothing intellectual to bring to the table. Black people have recounted experiences of not being consulted for suggestions on an important topic addressed in their workplace. There have also been cases where the work of Black people would have to be vetted by their white counterparts.

This assumption of intellectual inferiority is an obstacle to the upward mobility of a Black person in their organization.

Second-class citizenship and assumption of inferior status

Psychologists believe that the way an individual dresses affects the way they will be treated. If you wear designer suits, fancy ties, and designer shoes, you would be treated with respect, right? But what happens when your attire is negated based on just your skin color? Black workers are forced with trying to assimilate into white mainstream culture in order to fit in their workplaces, and the structure of the white spaces is one which fails to acknowledge the difficulty and the inherent stressors Black people are faced with in the predominantly white space.

For a Black individual, it is not enough that you wear a tie and put on a suit because that does little or nothing to change microaggressions you would face, which would at times lead to a more overt form of racism. Black people are automatically seen as second-class citizens in America, irrespective of whether they are putting on a suit or not. Tracy Ellis, a Black female attorney, in her TED Talk shared her experiences of being treated like a second-class citizen. She had gone to a courthouse, and like other attorneys, was waiting on the queue to check in with the clerks. There were two white attorneys in front of her, a male and a female. When it got to her turn, Ellis was not attended to by the clerk, but instead was directed to a different section of the courthouse meant for messengers. The clerk at the courthouse had overlooked the fact that Ellis was dressed professionally and was holding a yellow legal pad. What the clerk saw was just her skin color. A couple of years ago, two black men who were dressed in suits and were waiting at a Starbucks restaurant for their white business partner, were arrested by the police after the manager called the police. These two cases are among the several forms of discrimination Black people face in America. It is not enough that you are well dressed, because what people see is first your skin color before anything else. Reports have shown that on average it takes longer for a Black man to get a taxi compared to a white man. *The New York Times* reported a famous incident involving actor, Danny Glover. Glover was reported to have tried several times to get a taxi but to no avail. In other instances, he had to hide in the shadows while his daughter tried getting him a taxi, and when she had gotten one, the taxi driver had to be cajoled before he would open the door for Glover.

Black workers in corporate America are treated less compared to their white counterparts. Racial microaggressions in the workplace often involve white workers assuming that the Black workers in the organization are inferior to them. Black workers have been faced with instances when their white counterparts asked that the Black worker get them a cup of coffee or some other menial tasks. There is also the assumption that Black workers did not go to college, and for that those who managed to go to college, went only because of the principle of affirmative action.

Black workers are often passed over for job promotions, and for the few that manage to prove that they are worth promoting by doing double the work their white counterparts do, are still faced with subtle forms of discrimination where they often are faced with having to prove their humanity.

There are other cases where Black individuals who are holding either managerial or executive positions are assumed to be workers of less social status. When a white person sees a Black person, it is difficult to reconcile that this Black individual can be an accomplished individual and would immediately assume that the Black person is nothing more but a common worker. There have been cases where Black managers were assumed to not be managers and were met with shock when they introduced themselves as the manager. This occurrence might be explained by some individuals to be due to ignorance; however, this is beyond mere ignorance and instead a product of deep-seated racial biases.

Assumption of criminality

Will, a Black executive, was trying to park his car outside of his workplace when he heard a knock on his car window. He turned to find out who it was, and he discovered it was a white police officer. The police officer asked that Will get out of the car, and in typical fashion, like every Black person, Will came out with his hands in the air, careful to not agitate the officer. Will was wearing a black three-piece suit, but even this did not protect him from the assumption of being a criminal. There is also another incident of a professor getting arrested for breaking and entering his own apartment. It is not uncommon for Black customers in stores to be monitored closely and treated suspiciously by the storeowners. Whereas, white customers are not subjected to this form of treatment. Black people are more likely to be assumed shoplifters, and this occurs across all Black age groups and gender, regardless of how they were dressed.

The word Black has been shown by researchers to mean poor, violent, lazy, and dangerous. These labels are what an average white person sees when they encounter a Black person. The thing about microaggressions is that they are driven by unconscious or implicit bias, and this bias conflates being Black with being a criminal.

Being Black in America involves having to grapple with being mistaken for a criminal at every point without any evidence or fair hearing. The media's representation of Black people in stereotypical ways has done nothing to assuage these biases but has instead further entrenched them. It is quite 'normal' for a white woman to clutch her purse tightly as she walks by a Black person. This act of purse clutching is always reflexive and unconscious; however, for the Black man walking by a white woman and sees her clutching her purse on sighting him interprets her actions to mean she thinks of him as a threat. This assumption of criminality has been the basis for killings faced by Black people in present day America. A Black person is more likely to be pulled over by the police for random acts that otherwise would not have warranted stopping had the driver been white.

Assumed universality of the Black American experience

Many organizations pride themselves in having a single Black worker in the boardroom and often display this as proof of their diversity and openness. For a Black executive who looks around a room and sees only white faces, there often arises feelings of discomfort. It is not enough that organizations hire a single Black worker, and it also is not enough that the Black worker is seen as nothing more than a puppet to display to the world so the organization can provide proof of inclusion. There is the assumption that Black experiences are similar, and that a single Black person can speak for the multiple experiences of the Black race. This assumption erases the multiplicity and complexity of the Black race by reducing it to just similar experiences. Black workers are often faced with the burden of being experts on race and are faced with questions from their white counterparts on what is racially acceptable. This erases the singularity of the Black worker. In a predominantly white organization, Black workers are often consulted by their white counterparts on issues pertaining to just race but are ignored when it comes to more pivotal organizational decisions. In organizations that try to be racially inclusive, this might occur more as you reduce Black workers to just mere tools for the furtherance of their goal of being racially inclusive. This can be burdensome and predisposes the Black worker to pressure and stressors that would impede on their performance as workers. The undue ignoring of the expertise of Black workers in areas not based on race can be a source of mental distress, because the Black worker is made to feel less than their white counterparts.

Microaggression and gaslighting

Imagine fighting an enemy that only you can see but others cannot. You feel the effect. It comes at you like a thousand sharp blades and it tears your skin, leaving painful but invisible scars, and when you tell someone about it, they disregard it and tell you that what you are experiencing is not real. And that you should stop trying to draw attention to yourself and quit being a victim. This is what white America tells Black America when they complain about racism and microaggression. To them, since they do not see it and do not experience it, then it is not real.

Due to the subtle and covert nature of microaggression, most people are ignorant of it. A Black person might fall victim of microaggression and would have a gut feeling that they were treated the way they were treated because of their skin color. However, because the act of aggression was subtle and nonviolent, they begin to wonder if that action was racist or if they are being overly sensitive. There are some who believe that the term microaggression is one that was formulated so people belonging to minority groups can continue being victims. Some also believe that claims about microaggressions are just ways to stifle freedom of speech. This belief is an irony, seeing that people who were denied fundamental human rights were people of color and other members of minority groups. This need by some people to water down the experiences of Black people and tag them as overly sensitive not only seeks to erase the experiences of Black people, it also seeks to silence them and make them believe that they are delusional, which leads to many Black people choosing to remain quiet about their experiences with microaggressions. This thus leads to getting stuck in a cage of silence and paranoia, which has the capacity to result in grave psychological consequences such as depression, anxiety, and severe self-doubt.

The fact that white America does not see the negative effects of institutionalized racism and microaggression, does not in any way make it less real for the average Black person. There should not be an enforced silence when it comes to the issues of subtle racism, because even though these microaggressions can be regarded as subtle and invisible, their effects are real to those who experience it. So instead of trying to silence Black people and other minorities when they talk about their experiences with microaggression, white privileged America needs to listen, because before there can be solutions to any problem, there must be an acknowledgment that it exists.

CHAPTER FOUR

WHO AM I REALLY? CODE-SWITCHING IN CORPORATE AMERICA

I n a world where mainstream communication pattern is predominantly Eurocentric, African Americans are faced with the problem of adapting their speaking styles to fit into the western culture. For bilingual people, code-switching goes beyond mere imitating, but instead is a way of fitting into a broader culture that espouses the superiority of the white speaking pattern. A white child from young is taught to speak like a white person, and as they grow older, they do not have to worry if their way of speaking would be considered offensive by the next person. For the Black child however, this is not the case, as Black children from a young age are taught to code-switch when in predominantly white spaces. It is a rite of passage for young Black children to receive the talk from their parents on how to act around white people. There is the forced need for a Black person to censor certain parts of themselves because these parts are laden with negative stereotypes that strip the average Black person of their individuality and humanity.

This forces the average Black child to take on a form of duality. The Oreo or Coconut analogy paints this clearly. A Black person is expected to be Black on the outside and white on the inside. Black people are groomed to inhabit a double consciousness if they are to stand a chance in corporate America. Being white on the inside involves developing a taste for white style while rejecting Black style or way of life.

African American Vernacular English is regarded by white people to be an inferior dialect and is seen to be a product of an intellectually inferior mind. The beliefs that Black people are intellectually inferior made for the attachment of the inferior labels to anything of Black origin. This movement between the African American Vernacular English and the Standard American English is something for the Black mind to grapple with. Some might say that code-switching for Black people involves mere switching between languages, and that there is nothing inherently wrong with code-switching since non-Black people code-switch too. However, this claim fails to consider the decades of oppression meted out to Black people for wearing their identity proudly. For an average Black person, code-switching is a way of navigating the social world in a way that ensures your survival.

Code-Switching; beyond just verbal language

In a 2012, a viral clip of then President Obama in a men's locker room showed the president code-switch. There was a difference in the way he greeted the white coach and the way he greeted the Black basketball player. Most articles on code-switching cites President Obama as a good example of a Black person code-switching. An astute observer of Obama would notice the way he slips in and out of roles and mannerisms while giving speeches and interacting with different people. His speech patterns while talking to a white educated audience would be different from him talking with Black audiences.

Conventional definitions of code-switching conceptualize it to be limited to switching between language, dialects, and accents, but code-switching in contemporary America extends beyond just these. Code-switching extends to gestures, way of dressing, and other behavioral patterns.

Black people have adopted different ways of interacting with their fellow Black peers and with their white counterparts. Working as a Black individual in corporate America involves code-switching at every point. Some individuals do not even know when they code-switch because it has become natural to them. However, this practice of code-switching forces Black people to live in a contrived duality where they are always in the business of negotiating their humanity and validity by trying to fit into predominantly white spaces. Participants in a study admitted to adopting simpler versions of their name at work, just so it would be easier for their white counterparts to pronounce. This name simplification was not something they would have done ordinarily, but due to the requirement from white America for Black people to be less Black and less threatening, forced them to adopt simpler versions of their names. Some admitted to hearing from their white colleagues that names were too Black.

Code-switching extends to mannerism of speaking too. A Black worker is more likely to be perceived as less threatening if their manner of speaking was white. A Black high school teacher admitted to changing her speech pattern when in class and when interacting with the parents of her white students. Years ago, it would have been a thing of shock to even imagine a Black person being a teacher to white kids. Some Black teachers often feel the weight of the glares from some white parents who, if they had a choice, would not allow their white kids to be in the same room as a Black person, let alone allow that Black person to teach their kids. For Black teachers, changing their speech patterns and gestures is needed just so they could be perceived as intellectually competent enough to teach white kids. There are other teachers, especially college professors, who decided to not censor their way of speaking because that to them would be a denial of their identity and would be an admittance to white citizens that the Black way of speaking is inherently bad. Their choice to not censor themselves did not come without consequences, but to them, they as intellectuals needed to dismantle and not reinforce white supremacy and Black inferiority.

Black workers in corporate America approximate their speech patterns to align with the white standard of speaking in the workplace. The complexity of code-switching in corporate America is such that makes Black workers erase important parts of their identity to prevent their white counterparts from feeling uncomfortable. This is scarcely a question of trying to align with workplace standards. Code-switching for Black employees in corporate America stems from the stereotypes attached to Black mannerisms. A Black worker must adopt a whiter style of dressing while at work and while around white colleagues. The problem with this is that corporate America is modeled after white Eurocentric standards which exemplifies the way of life of just a single group, which in this case is the white majority. This structure keeps minorities out and ensures that they can only be accepted into that space if they are willing to assimilate into the prevailing white standards and drop their personalities and way of life at the gate. Making African Americans conform to workplace standards, which are actually Eurocentric standards, is inevitably forcing Black employees into reneging on their own culture. The work environment is structured such that a Black way of living cannot exist with Eurocentric workplace standards, due to the negative stereotypes attached to being Black.

The ability of a Black worker to code-switch has been shown to be tied to their wellbeing, economic advancement, and physical survival. Being in corporate America and having the weight of stereotypical expectations hanging over one like a scepter leads to the need to self-preserve by conforming. In the short run, code-switching can help a Black worker ease the anxiety that comes with being labeled and placed in a box. By adapting your speech, gestures, and dressing to align with workplace standards, Black workers can fluidly get into another persona which offers them acceptance and hence lessens feelings of being an outsider. However, in the long run, this can lead to emotional exhaustion and burnout as studies have shown that creating a façade of conformity leads to emotional exhaustion. Daily inhabiting of multiple identities and never having the freedom to be yourself can be detrimental to the mental health of an individual.

Code- Switching, the power dynamics of it

Is there anything inherently wrong in trying to fit your behavior to align with the norm of society? Some individuals might say that code-switching is not limited to just racial minorities and that white people also code-switch at times when interacting with certain individuals. Individuals adopt different speech patterns while communicating with different individuals. We adopt a more formal language when talking to a superior at work. We talk a different way with our parents and different ways with our friends. These all are forms of code-switching. However, code switching among Black people and racial minorities goes beyond just merely adopting a different speech pattern or gestures but is instead laden with a history of racial oppression.

For there to be an objective analysis of code-switching, we need to look at the power dynamics prevalent in code-switching. For an average Black person, switching from African American English is not merely a matter of trying to adhere to the social norms, but is instead a way of trying to fit into a society that demonizes African American English. Linguists have discovered that African American English possesses its own grammatical and phonetic rules and can be studied as a valid language of speaking. African American English is an important part of the Black identity with roots in West Africa. Black people were brought as slaves to America, and with this transition, came the severance of African American roots to its African heritage. The evolution of African American English occurred such that Black people were able to merge their African roots with the language of the society they now lived in, to create a language that was solely theirs. This language, however, was seen to be inferior to the standard American English, and Black people were forced to conform to the standard American English in order to be accepted into American society.

Black people in America are burdened with having to be viewed by non-Blacks through harmful and negative stereotypical lens. Speaking AAE is seen as an indicator of the inferior status of the average Black person. There is also the issue of Black people being seen as averagely violent and aggressive, and thus speaking in what is considered Black manner is seen as a threat and makes white people be on the defensive.

Take for instance, a white person adopting mannerisms that would be regarded as Black mannerisms. A white person can adopt the Black way of speaking and dressing and would face less discrimination at the hands of their white counterparts. This goes to show that there is nothing inherently wrong with the typical Black way of speaking, but the problem lies with the stereotypes attached to it, which makes the speaker be seen as violent and aggressive just because of their skin color.

A study surveyed a group of American and African American women on code-switching. The first group which was predominantly white, felt code-switching was a choice and was a marker of emotional intelligence. For this group, the ability to adapt your language and tone of speaking was an important tool, and that they could choose to code-switch. For the other group that consisted mainly of African American women, code-switching was mandatory to their survival. One was quoted to have mentioned how her professor at college had said to her that she was Black, and that she needed to smile more when speaking, so as to not come off as threatening. This, however, was not the reason the white women code-switch.

For Black people, code-switching was important to their survival in the American corporate world. Studies have shown that the whiter a person speaks, the higher their chances at being perceived as genuine. This of course had nothing to do with the content of their speech but merely the way they spoke and the gestures they made while speaking. Speaking in a high pitch and adopting slower cadences by Black people was essential for their survival. In a TED Talk video by Chandra Arthur, a Black woman, she talked about an encounter she had with local law enforcement. She had returned home and was arranging her things. There was no car outside of the house, and her white neighbor heard noises from the house and called the police to report a burglary. The local law enforcement arrived, and Chandra was asked to step out of the house while their guns were pointed at her. In her talk, she mentioned that her ability to code-switch saved her life that day. What if the person could not code-switch, she asked in the video?

In corporate America or in the office, there is no law enforcement with a gun pointed at you. But there is the jeer from co-workers. Black workers have had experiences where clients requested to be allowed to interface with someone else that was not Black. Survival in corporate America for an average Black person involves code-switching to get access to opportunities.

A study revealed that Black workers who have high leadership ambitions felt more pressure to code-switch, because the chances of climbing up the social ladder is slimmer for the average Black man. Hence, if you want to survive in the world of business and entrepreneurship, you must filter out the Blackness.

Code-switching in the words of W.E.B DuBois creates a form of racial schizophrenia where you do not know who you are. Being forced to juggle double identities which is believed to not be able to co-exist, sets you in a situation where you are neither here nor there. Black people who have been habituated to code-switching are not strangers to hearing remarks from their Black counterparts that they have whitewashed themselves. There is the struggle of navigating double spaces while trying to reconcile your sense of who you are in spaces where you might not be fully accepted.

There is a great divide within several top work sectors and various fields of study for African American men and women who feel the need to maintain one persona when addressing and interacting with their white colleagues, so as not to come across as angry and aggressive. This need to police and censor oneself can contribute to one's feelings of depression, and in some rare occasions, have contributed to one's desire to commit self-harm. Code-switching, even though necessary for Black people's survival in the short run, can have negative psychological and emotional consequences for them in the long run. Constantly having to change or censor yourself, even though it can protect you and provide a semblance of acceptance, would accumulate into harmful and detrimental health effects for the average Black person in corporate America.

Code-switching in itself is not bad, as some Black people have put forward that code-switching should be seen as their superpower and not as a Kryptonite. However, what if there exists a world where Black people do not have to feel pressured to code-switch? What if the decision to code switch is one that a Black person on their own accord chooses and not because their survival depends on it? And what if we as humans evolve past racial biases and divorce those negative stereotypes attached to being Black from an individual's identity and how we perceive them?

CHAPTER FIVE

OVERCOMING IMPOSTER SYNDROME

I magine being in a room where the majority of people in the room with you perceive you to be less intelligent, less civilized, prone to anger and aggression, and more likely to be a criminal. You of course would want to try to prove that you are not these things and that they are mistaken about you. Now add to this scenario the fact that you have a presentation to make in that boardroom and that most if not all are subtly expecting you to fail, or are basically looking for cues to align with their perception of you. Being aware of this can cause you to spend time worrying about ways to not make yourself conform to stereotypes, instead of actually spending time working on your presentation. Self-doubt begins to creep in, and you wonder if you deserve to be in that space at all. This is what psychologists refer to as imposter syndrome. It is an intense feeling of self-doubt stemming from the insecurity about not being good enough and believing that you are a fraud. The interesting thing about imposter syndrome is that most of the time, the feelings of self-doubt are not rooted in facts but are just functions of an individual's perception.

Several individuals are prone to experiencing imposter syndrome at different points in their lives. There were times when I was in a room filled with people who I felt were better than I was, and I was overcome with an intense desire to leave that room because I believed I did not earn my space in that room. I was supposed to make a presentation, but instead, I spent the entire time leading up to the presentation worrying about what I would say and how I would say it. I did not want to come across as inexperienced and not good enough. I put myself in a cage where I was not allowed to make mistakes. Take for instance the story about Jamal, a young Black man looking to be an entrepreneur. Jamal always envisioned himself being a business owner due to being exposed to the idea of entrepreneurship by various family members and friends who owned restaurants, real estate companies, as well as a tax preparation company. He was always good at assisting others with navigating through the process of becoming a homeowner as a result of watching his mother work in the real estate field, as well as hearing many discussions she would have with her clients. Many would consider Jamal as the go-to guy for solving various problematic issues. Most of the people that Jamal's mother assisted were typically experiencing financial hardships, and she would assist many of her clients with credit repair services in an effort to find the funding to purchase a home. He knew most of the owners of third-party businesses that she would refer her clients to, to assist them with securing the funding to buy their first home. Jamal figured that he would start a consulting firm to assist in solving people's problems. His efforts in networking and promoting his services led him to obtaining a client who was a well-known politician in his city, running for a seat in the senate. Jamal began to ruminate over the idea of not being good enough because this was his first client. The client, however, did not know this. Jamal committed himself to researching the individual in an effort to obtain as much background information on him. Jamal was able to talk with the client, and during their conversation, the client mentioned that he perceived Jamal to be a confident person and that he believed Jamal could do the Job. However, Jamal felt otherwise. In his own words he said, "I am really relying on the 'fake it until you make it' theory and afraid that I would be exposed as a fraud!"

Jamal believed that he was simply faking being confident, and that sooner or later, the client would perceive him to be a fraud. This constant rumination about being exposed as a fraud led to a depletion of Jamal's cognitive resources, which made him all the more anxious. This persuaded him to call the client and tell him that he could not do what was required of him.

Jamal's story is not a new one. Many people with imposter syndrome are familiar with how their insecurity and self-doubt led to them engaging in self-sabotaging behaviors.

Women and minority groups are more likely to be victims of imposter syndrome, and this stems largely from the negative stereotypes attached to the group. If you are in a room where most of the people there are different from you and are members of the majority, you as a minority will likely feel threatened by their expectations of you. You believe that it is your duty to prove that you deserve to be in that room, that you deserve to prove your worth to them.

In spaces filled with predominantly white workers, a Black worker is more likely to be faced with feelings of inferiority. Black people have less access to places of influence, and for those who worked their way up the professional ladder, they still feel insufficient based on their belief that they only got to where they are because they were lucky and not that they deserved it. An average Black worker in a predominantly white space is likely to believe that there are other Black workers like him out there who are doing the hard work but are yet excluded from these spheres of influence. This puts an unnecessary strain on the worker.

Imposter syndrome is inextricably linked to stereotype threats. Stereotype threats occur in situations where one expects that they would be judged based on their membership to a group, and especially if that group is laden with burdens of stereotypes. Studies have shown that African Americans were more likely to fail a standardized test if they were told that most African Americans failed that test. This is because the individual, instead of investing cognitive resources into the tasks, invests it in worrying about his performance, which leads to performance anxiety, and thus impairs their performance.

Imposter Syndrome and the cage of expectations

Imagine having to live in a world where at every point, you are burdened with having to prove your worth as a person.

That would be daunting and would surely impede on your performance because you would always try to be on your best behavior. Navigating productivity involves allowing yourself room to make mistakes. If you are so focused on being perfect, you would find it hard to do what is required of you. Mistakes allow us to learn how to be better, but there is a world where making mistakes is not a luxury some people can afford. Racial minorities and gender minorities are examples of such group.

Imposter syndrome is characterized by persistent anxiety about standards. Studies have shown that people suffering from imposter syndrome have a gnawing desire to be perfect, thus setting unrealistic standards for themselves that allow no room for flexibility. For Black workers in corporate America, this need for perfection tends to make them rigid and less creative, thus hampering their productivity. One important factor needed for creativity and problem solving is flexibility in thinking. To be able to find solutions to problems, you must allow yourself to see from different perspectives. However, as an individual, burdened with the desire to be perfect, there will be no room for flexibility in thinking, as your cognitive resources will be spent on trying to avoid making mistakes in order to not confirm the negative stereotypes people have about you.

A study on imposter syndrome sought out to answer the question of whether those with imposter syndrome react as they are expected to when they know they are being observed by strangers. Participants were subjected to two different experimental conditions. In the first condition, the participants were made to believe that they were being observed positively, and in the other condition, participants were made to believe they were being observed negatively. The results showed that participants were more likely to perform better when they believed they were being observed positively and were more likely to perform poorly when they believed that they were being observed negatively.

Having an awareness that you are expected to fail can lead to you failing. However, there have been studies that showed that when individuals were aware of the negative stereotypes and expectations others have about them, they were more likely to want to prove the expectations wrong and hence did perform better. This, however, came at a high cost.

Due to the stereotypes attached to being Black, an average Black person is forced to walk on eggshells, trying not to do anything that would be seen in negative light. This leads to an overconcentration on being the best version of yourself and editing out parts of you that would fit into the stereotypical expectations. The ability to be yourself and allow yourself to make mistakes is essential for success in any endeavor. However, being burdened with the need to be perfect at all points can lead to feelings of insecurity.

Corporate America is designed in a way that favors white individuals over their Black counterparts and ensures that Black employees have less access to opportunities. This is evident in the number of Black people in well-paying jobs, even though they make up a sizeable amount of the population. In the first chapter of this book, we examined the racial inequalities in well-paying jobs and places of influence in America. A Black college graduate is less likely to get a job that utilizes his full potential, and what might be the cause of this? You guessed right, stereotypes and expectations.

In psychology, there is a concept called self-fulfilling prophecy, and as the name suggests, it is a prophecy that fulfills itself. This occurs in situations where an individual has certain expectations of another individual, and this individual by reason of these expectations acts a certain way while interacting with the individual. If you believe an individual is aggressive, you would expect that at every chance they get, they would act aggressive. This would invariably make you be on the defensive, and thus see their actions that otherwise would not be regarded as aggressive to be a reflection of their aggression. The interesting thing about this is that your expectation of them being aggressive would make you act in a provocative way towards them, which would then lead to them being aggressive, hence the prophecy fulfills itself.

If you expect that an individual will not do well in a certain task, this belief will make you put less effort in ensuring that they do well in that task. Instead, your actions which are being fueled by your implicit bias would impede on their ability to perform well on the task. There have been studies that showed that Black students were recorded to fail more when their teachers had lower expectations of them. The lower expectations prevented the teachers from going the extra mile to ensure that the students had a good grasp of the subject matter. The teacher would hence attribute the student's failures to be a true reflection of their abilities.

Growing up Black involves contending with these expectations every day. No one expects that a Black person thrives in corporate America. Some might be quick to cite the low numbers of Black executives in corporate America to be an indicator of the true reality, while ignoring the structural difficulties in place that have ensured that few Black people climb up the social ladder.

Having a few numbers of successful Black people in corporate America is not reflective of America being a land of opportunities, but it reflects the lack of access that they have in corporate America. An average Black man is not expected to dream big because dreaming big is for people with access to opportunities who are not burdened with society's expectations of them. There exists a prevalence of implicit bias against Black people in the structure of corporate America that makes upward mobility difficult for them.

Imposter Syndrome and Tokenism

Due to the low representation of Black people in corporate America, there exists a scarcity of role models that younger Black people can chart their lives after. And for those who manage to work their way into corporate America, there is that feeling that they got there due to either affirmative action or due to the fact that the organization wants to boast of employing a Black worker.

Tokenism refers to the belief that the things you have achieved as an individual were handed out to you due to some reasons external to you, not particularly because you worked hard for it or deserved it. For members of the minority, this belief that your achievements were gifted to you is pervasive. An average successful Black person with track records of achievement might be likely to still doubt themselves and believe that they were successful just because they were lucky, and that sooner or later would be found out to be a fraud. Maya Angelou is quoted to have said that even after writing eleven books, that there were times she believed that she would be found out to be a fraud.

Growing up Black means looking at the spheres of influence for people with similar features as yourself but finding only a small number of people. Stevon Lewis, a Black male therapist, shared his experience with imposter syndrome. According to him, there were no examples to follow or model himself after, and this led to him doubting and questioning his ability. He wondered if he ever was going to be successful as a Black male therapist. This is one of the several instances where the lack of adequate models in well-paying and respected jobs in America leads to the lack of interest of young college graduates venturing into that field despite having the qualifications.

There have been cases where Black workers hear that the only reason they went to college was because of affirmative action and not that they deserved it. An average Black worker tends to internalize this and believes that it is a true reflection of reality.

This leads to feelings of worthlessness and insecurity, which translates into the imposter syndrome phenomenon. Like it was mentioned earlier, many people across ages, gender, and race experience imposter syndrome; however, the mechanism through which racial minorities come to develop imposter syndrome differs due to structural deficiencies rooted in racial stereotypes.

Overcoming Imposter syndrome; beyond just individual decision

Mainstream methods of combatting imposter syndrome espouse the use of different techniques by the individual. One way to achieve this is to talk to someone about the feelings of self-doubt and insecurity in order to get their perspective about your performance. This has been shown to help lessen feelings of being an imposter. Having someone point out the areas eaten up by your blind spots can help you gain clarity about your actual performance. Like it was noted earlier, imposter syndrome is often rooted in a subjective reality driven by our insecurity and the unrealistic expectations we set for ourselves, which is sometimes a function of the expectations of others.

CHAPTER SIX

CORPORATE TRAUMA:
Exploring how CTSD and cognitive dissonance play a significant role within the Black identity and one's experience in corporate America and the world of entrepreneurship.

P ost-traumatic stress disorder (PTSD) is a recognized mental health disorder and occurs in response to a traumatic incident. For people who have been exposed to a shocking, scary, or dangerous event, there is a likelihood of developing PTSD. Initial cases of PTSD were observed to occur among veteran soldiers who had been to war and those who were victims of rape. However, there has been new research which points to the fact that racism can cause PTSD. Monica Williams, a clinical psychologist, mentioned that daily exposure to microaggressions can cause symptoms of PTSD among Black people. African Americans have been shown to have a higher prevalent rate for PTSD compared to white people. Williams mentioned that one in ten Black people becomes traumatized. This rate could surely be higher as research limitations could obfuscate the actual prevalence. In the general population of Black people, experiences of racism can lead to great psychological distress which has the potential to hamper daily activities and hence lessen productivity. Constant exposure to racist attacks has devastating consequences for the average Black person. Studies have shown that an average Black person is likely to report more feelings of paranoia, which lead to them being overly vigilant as they believe that everyone is likely to be against them.

Research has shown that repeated exposure to images of violence against Black people can overtime accumulate into symptoms of PTSD, even if you never experienced the violence yourself. Images of Black men being killed by police can be triggering and lead to grave psychological distress. Due to the history of oppression meted out on Black people, there is an increased priming by Black people to experience discrimination based on their racial identity. Even though you might not have been exposed to discrimination or overt violence, an awareness that someday you might fall victim can lead to feelings of distress. In the Black community, it is no longer surprising to hear about the killings of young Black men and women by white police officers for random acts that did not warrant the killing.

News like this is peddled as bedtime stories among the average Black family, because survival means priming yourself for what some might regard as the inevitable. This vigilance and constant need to always look over one's shoulder puts the average Black person in the fight or flight mode, which of course has high detrimental health effects. PTSD is often regarded to be a response to a singular traumatic event, and the symptoms are expected to diminish after a few months. However, due to the persistent nature of racial discrimination and violence against Black citizens, there is no end to the exposure to these situations.

Corporate Traumatic Stress Disorder

Aside from the traumatic experiences Black people are forced to deal with as they navigate their existence in the world, there is also the problem of stress at work, largely due to their identity as African American. Stress is not entirely negative, as studies have shown that stress is an integral part of human life. However, prolonged exposure to stressful situations, especially when the situation overwhelms the body's capacity to cope, can have detrimental effects.

The World Health Organization (WHO), in their guideline on work-related stress, defined a healthy job as "one where the pressures on employees are appropriate in relation to their abilities and resources to the amount of control they have over their work, and to the support they receive from people who matter to them." This definition emphasizes the proportion of pressure put on employees and their ability and resources to cope. When an individual's ability to cope with pressure is diminished, it can lead to harmful health outcomes. There is also the importance of perceived social support in coping with stress. Research has shown the link between burnout and perceived social support. An individual is less likely to report burnout if he perceives that he has enough social support.

The World Health Organization in their guideline further defines health to not merely be the absence of disease or infirmity but a positive state of physical, mental, and social wellbeing. A healthy working environment according to the WHO is one in which there is not only the absence of harmful conditions, but also the abundance of health promoting ones.

The need for affiliation is an important human need. No one likes being regarded as an outsider, so even in predominantly white spaces, a Black person still feels the need to belong, and when this need is not fulfilled, it can lead to feelings of distress. We like seeing ourselves in a positive light, and we also like others to see us in a positive light too. Racial discrimination thrives on the perceived inferiority of the racial minority and the espousal of the superior status of white people. This leads to the otherwise inhumane treatment of Black people by those who espouse the racial superiority of white individuals. In corporate America, racial discrimination manifests itself in microaggressions as discussed in the previous chapter.

These microaggressions can lead to the average Black worker distancing himself from those who are a source of discomfort and negative evaluation. At times and due to the paranoia that comes with being subjected to these traumatic stressors at work, the Black worker distances himself from almost all his co-workers, thereby becoming socially isolated at work.

Studies have shown that social isolation and lack of social support are associated with psychological distress, higher morbidity, and lower life expectancies. The average life expectancy of Black people is lesser than the average life expectancies of white people. A study on life expectancy based on level of education, found that Black people with college degrees have a lower life expectancy than their white counterparts. The study also found that Black high school dropouts had higher life expectancies than Black college graduates. This is partly due to the discrimination faced by Black people who attend college. Black college students face constant discrimination from peers and professors. This continues into the work life, hence affecting their health. An average Black worker is faced with the stressors that work ordinarily subjects someone to, and in addition, is faced with stressors that emanate from racial discrimination.

Studies have shown that high level of discrimination is associated with higher risk of developing high blood pressure, obesity, heart complications, and even premature mortality. Black people die from the effects of direct racial discrimination which manifests itself in overt acts of violence against them. And even if as an individual, you do not fall victim to these overt acts of violence, microaggressions in the workplace and exposure to videos and images of violence against Black people can also impact your mental and physical health.

Corporate traumatic stress disorder (CTSD) is not a recognized mental health disorder; however, there is the possibility of a situation where work environment can be a source of stress for individuals that could translate into experiences of trauma. There have been reports about the harmful and toxic nature of corporate America for those belonging to minority groups. Workplace sexual harassment against women is on the increase, and due to structural deficiencies, most women are forced to remain working in a toxic environment. For racial minorities, there is the issue of workplace discrimination stemming from their identity as racial minorities. In the preceding chapters, the prevalence of microaggressions against Black employees in corporate America and constant exposure to remarks that are considered derogatory can lead to symptoms of traumatic stress disorder. Studies have shown that there is a high rate of discrimination induced PTSD among African Americans. The average Black worker often does not get recognition or respect from their white counterparts or their supervisors. It is not uncommon to see a Black worker being mistreated and subjected to open or indirect attacks, ridicule, and derogation. These social stressors have been shown to be associated with the development of symptoms of PTSD.

Cognitive dissonance and the riddle of Black identity

When watching old films from the early 1900s with African American actors, we see how the portrayal of such actors was that of a passive and docile demeanor. As we fast forward to the 1950s-70s, we see an uprising in cultural respect and love for who we truly are and what we bring to the table. But for many, there continues to be a distortion in their views as to how they have been taught to conduct themselves in the work environment and in society. This distortion causes a direct conflict in learned behaviors, core values, and existing beliefs of one's identity. This distortion causes a cognitive dissonance and typically shows up as feelings of forced compliance and changes in dissonant beliefs, which begins to reduce the significance of one's core belief.

In the chapter on code-switching, we examined how this skill is a vital tool for a Black person navigating corporate America. The ability to act and talk white and to divorce certain parts of yourself is what corporate White America requires of Black people before they could be given a seat at the table. This, however, creates tension within the individual as he or she is being forced to act out a role and be what he is not.

Cognitive dissonance was put forward by Leon Festinger, and it refers to the tension that arises when an individual has two or more conflicting beliefs or hears two or more conflicting messages on how to conduct themselves. In America, cognitive dissonance occurs among Black citizens when they are forced to reconcile who they are and who society requires them to be. There are Black people who have tried to assimilate into white culture and feel they do not belong in either the Black community or white community. This requirement by white people for Black people to be more civilized, which means they should act more like white people, creates a form of racial hybrid that has no sense of belonging neither here nor there. This is a manifestation of the cognitive dissonance faced by Black people in corporate America.

An average Black person who manages to get into a predominantly white college might hear from his parents to not lose their Blackness; however, the key to being successful in that space is based on the level at which you can tone down on your Blackness because your Blackness is seen as a threat. This leads to a sense of displacement, which invariably affects the sense of identity of a Black person.

Is America not the land that emphasizes being oneself at every point in time and that knowing and being proud of who you are is a needed ingredient for success? Most movies tend to portray how staying true to your values and identity is important for success, as it keeps you grounded and tethered. Apparently, this message applies only to the white person. It is safe to say that these movies and the messages they portray tend to revolve around the white identity. And I am not trying to make anyone the villain here. Instead, what I am trying to do is raise our awareness as to how America sends its citizens the message that an individual needs to be proud of their heritage on one hand, and on the other, causes the average Black person to not be proud of who they are. This goes to show that those messages about being proud of who you are were not constructed with the Black person in mind. When a Black person watches that movie and hears that message and decides that his identity as a Black person is something he should be proud of and decides to do just that, when he gets out there in the real world, he discovers that America would only accept him if he tones down his Blackness and becomes more white. This leads to tension within self, because how can he reconcile these two messages which are evidently at odds with each other?

A study found that Black people who have a solid sense of identity and are proud about being Black tend to be less predisposed to developing racism induced post-traumatic stress disorder. Having a solid Black identity is a factor that moderates the negative psychological and emotional effects of racial discrimination. Psychologists have studied the importance of self-acceptance for the mental and overall wellbeing of individuals. Accepting yourself is an important factor for overall mental and physical wellbeing. Self-acceptance involves being proud of yourself as an individual despite your shortcoming, as being human means being flawed. Our self-identity is inextricably linked to our group identity. Being a part of a group involves identifying with the group, and due to a sense of belonging you derive from that group, you take negative comments about that group to heart. Toning down your Blackness involves divorcing and distancing yourself from the group you belong to, and this can lead to feelings of social alienation which has been shown to have negative consequences on the emotional and psychological wellbeing of any individual.

However, there exists a conundrum for a Black individual in corporate America. As discussed earlier in this chapter, being Black in a predominantly white space has a harmful effect on your mental and physical wellbeing, and one way for you as a Black person to manage this is by having a solid sense of identity. What this means is that the protective factor against racial discrimination is you being proud of your identity as a Black person. The irony of this is that you are expected to do away with this thing that can shield you from the negative effect of racism. This, therefore, is the riddle of the Black identity in corporate America. You can either shed your skin, which is a protective factor, or you can embrace it. The dissonance lies in how to reconcile this desire to be successful in corporate America and not losing your sense of self. Looking at this critically, you would realize that the system is 'rigged' to ensure that the average Black person does not win. Because even if you manage to tone down your Blackness just so you can climb up the social ladder, that does not mean that you will be accepted fully by white America. And this could lead to you feeling like a sellout because you think you have thrown away the core of your being, which leads to feelings of isolation.

CTSD and cognitive dissonance both work together to bring about grave psychological and emotional consequences for the average Black person. As we know it today, in the future, diagnoses of PTSD arising from working environments will no doubt lead to some interesting employment law cases. Although CTSD is not a recognized disorder at this time, we cannot deny the existence of symptoms that are due to working in corporate America, especially among members of minority groups. What if CTSD becomes a recognized anxiety disorder? This could lead to major corporations becoming prospects of large class action lawsuits for CTSD, which would lead to a fundamental change in the way these corporations operate. It is not enough to claim to be racially diverse or have a few persons of color among your employees. There is the need for corporate America to examine the many ways in which it contributes to racial discrimination of their workers of color and then implementing the necessary policies that would protect these workers from feelings of tension that arise just for deciding to affirm their identity.

CHAPTER SEVEN

LET US BRING IT ALL TOGETHER

Thriving While Black sets out to explore the psychological and emotional consequences of being Black in corporate America. Racism is an institutional problem, pervading almost all spheres of life for a Black person. There cannot be a conversation about being Black and thriving while Black without an exploration of the many factors that impede on this. From the start, Black people have been discriminated against and excluded based on their skin color, and this has ensured that they remain at the lower rung of the ladder. Institutionalized racism is pervasive in corporate America. Over the past few years, there has been an increase in the number of Black people in the middle class. We see today's middle class to be composed of Black businessmen and women, lawyers, doctors, schoolteachers, and others. There has also been a reduction in the number of people who are overtly racist. Some might say that America is in a post-racist era, given the fact that Black citizens have access to opportunities. This, however, is partially true. Institutionalized racism was studied by Stokely Carmichael and Charles Hamilton in the 1960s, and they found that there still exists persistent Black inequalities in the structural makeup of America. They highlighted that an average white person, regardless of motivation and behavior, and whether they were racists or not, benefited from social structures and organizational patterns that have continually put the average Black person at a disadvantage. The playing field for Black and white people is not equal.

Black people are also burdened with the trauma of slavery and the Jim Crow laws, and this has set the average Black person back, impeding on their ability to thrive. We cannot talk about the experiences of the average Black person without talking about the historical factors that burden the average Black person. The dehumanization of Black people during slavery is but a shackle that still lies in the background, sneaking up on us and making us question our place in America. There is still several decades of oppression that manifests itself still in today's America. There still exists a belief that white people are better than Black people, and the espousal of being a post-racist society does not change the fact that Black people are not yet seen as equal to white people. The average white college graduate still earns more than the average Black college graduate. Most highly educated Black people are still less likely to be employed than their white counterparts, and for those that manage to secure job positions in corporate America, they either receive less pay compared to their white counterparts or are underutilized, as they are made to work in positions that do not require a college degree.

The underutilization and underemployment of Black people in corporate America has led to the lack of adequate Black representation. The lack of Black representation in spheres of influence has made it even more difficult for Black people to aspire to those positions, as they see those spaces as not inclusive to Black people. There is also the issue of the intentional erasure of the contribution of Black people to the field of science and technology, and this is due to the implicit bias that Black people cannot be smart. Black people who showed interest in education during the slave era were regarded as an aberration and abnormal. For the Black person, it is difficult to reconcile the belief that Black people were intellectually inferior, with the image of a Black person showing promise in science and technology. This creates a form of cognitive dissonance in the average white person, and to resolve that dissonance, they make themselves believe that the Black person was nothing but an aberration. And due to this exclusion of Black people from the field of science and technology, there exists a scarcity of Black historical figures that the average Black child can identify with. What this creates is the belief that Black people are not inherently built to excel in those fields.

In the words of Langston Hughes, Ain't I an American? This is a question every Black person even without knowing asks themselves. Ain't we Americans? Ain't we humans? Before we even talk about our identity as Americans, we need to question whether America sees us as humans. There was a protest in America after the killing of George Floyd by a white police officer and captions about Black Lives Matter were all over the internet. When will America realize that Black lives do matter? And that we should not have to negotiate our right to live through protests.

There exists in America the unequal treatment of unequal people. The humanity of a group of people should not be something to be reduced to mere negative stereotypes. The impact of slavery on the Black psyche is not something that has been done away with.

We need to come to the realization that the negative stereotypes attached to the Black person are nothing but mere symptoms of a deficient system, and what this does is create a situation where the Black person's quest to demand respect from society is seen as violent and aggressive. There exists a perpetual cycle that keeps Black people in cages of societal expectation, and this has in a way led to the internalization of these expectations by Black people, which results in them acting out those expectations. Identity they say is a function of how others see us. Individuals form their sense of self through the lens of society. The Black identity in the lens of society is one laden with negative stereotypes, so when an average Black child looks through this lens for a sense of identity, sees only the image of himself as aggressive, intellectually inferior, and poor. The Black child thus believes this to be his or her reality, and this creates a form of a psychological cage for the average Black child. There was an image on the internet of a police officer asking a Black girl what she wanted to be when she grows up. "Alive," the girl replies. She just wants to be alive. Having an awareness that a day would come when you as a Black person might fall victim to police brutality can make one less likely to want to dream or be ambitious. Research has shown that the average Black person has a lower life expectancy than the average white person. Every seven minutes a Black person in America dies. Do Black lives not matter?

I should not have to assimilate to be accepted

Acceptance should not have to be conditional. The desire of white America for an average Black person to assimilate, as discussed in the preceding chapter, comes from the implicit belief about the superior status of the white person. America is a country with more white people, and thus the white way of life is mainstream and other ethnicities or races need to adopt this white way of life before they can be accepted into society. This need, however, is a threat to American diversity, which is ironic because America seems to pride itself in being a land of diversity and opportunities. In America, however, the level of acceptance and opportunities a person of color gets is dependent on their willingness to become white. The implicit bias of White America against people of color is in part a result of their need to be the center of the world. History has shown how Black people who have made immense contribution to the American economy were erased from the history books. Records have shown that Black business owners are a source of employment for many Americans, but the mainstream ideas about Black people is one where they are lazy and unemployed. This need to see Black America as monolithic is cognitively lazy because it refuses to admit that even in the Black community, there exists diversity. There is no one way to be Black, and White America needs to be aware of this and stop clinging onto harmful and unfounded stereotypes that have for years been propagated by people who felt threatened by the average Black person. Black people are Americans too and should not have to be less and unequal.

There is no denying the harmful effects of trying to police and censor yourself as discussed in the preceding chapters. Changing who you are in order to be accepted has been shown to have harmful psychological consequences for an individual. American mainstream culture is predominantly white; however, there should not be a forced need for Black people to adopt mainstream white culture while neglecting their own African American identity. The beauty about diversity is not gathering different and diverse people and trying to make them act the same way, but instead bringing diverse people into the room and allowing their diversity to thrive. This should be the focus of America. There needs to be an increased awareness about the negative and harmful effects of racism in America, and white people should also see how their privilege might make them blind to the reality of the average Black person.

ABOUT THE AUTHOR

Cori J. Williams MSW L.C.S.W

Cori Williams MSW L.C.S.W is a graduate from the prestigious Boston University located in the heart of Boston Massachusetts. A multifaceted entrepreneur, Cori is the owner of Wilmore Marketing Consultants LLC. a Marketing Firm out of Atlanta Ga. offering Internet Marketing Solutions for consumers and business owners. In his latest endeavor as an Executive Life Coach, he is the founder of Quintessential Wellness Solutions LLC., a Family Therapy & Executive Life Coaching Practice and Co-Owner of B&M Enterprises which is a real estate investors Company.

Before his entrepreneurial success, Williams worked in the Nonprofit industry for 12 years holding various leadership roles. In his career years, he assisted with establishing GED curriculum workshop for adult learners and facilitated numerous workshops for first-time fathers who struggle with maintaining consistency in the lives of their children and face social and emotional barriers which has prevented them from consistently engaging in the lives of their children in the urban communities.

Having transitioned into the coaching industry, he takes it upon himself to wholeheartedly use his experience to serve people. As an Executive Life coach, he works with professionals and individuals to identify their strengths. Working with career professionals and business owners, Mr. Williams helps them identify their business strengths and weaknesses to propel these regardless of the industry they service. Furthermore, he assists them in identifying and executing solutions to their problems. He also works with them to rebuild their confidence, purpose and drive to succeed in life. With his experience, these clients can also overcome emotional barriers that has prevented them from creating the impact in life and their professional world, showcasing their natural capabilities.

However, Mr. Williams finds his career paths to be abundantly rewarding and within his capabilities shares valuable experience to his clients. Whether in the corporate field, business, or wellness, he finds strength in seeing individuals thrive and living a life of purpose. Cori is inspired by the renowned Civil Rights Leader Dr. Martin Luther King Jr. Besides coaching and entrepreneurship, he has co-authored academic journals and wellness/reentry curriculums focusing on reducing recidivism within the urban communities. Mr. Williams has also partnered with many well-established business professionals offering Coaching courses on Mindset Shifting for the purpose of prepping aspiring investors and business startups in effort to assist individuals with beginning the process of starting generational wealth.